Marching Smithereens

Written by ANN HAYES

Illustrated by KARMEN THOMPSON

HARCOURT BRACE & COMPANY   San Diego   New York   London

Many thanks to WILLIAM KEARNS, Professor of Music,
and TOM CANEVA, Associate Director of Bands,
at the University of Colorado at Boulder.
Thanks also to STEVE CHRISTOPHER, Director of Bands
at Fairview Senior High School, Boulder.
—A. H. and K. T.

Library of Congress Cataloging-in-Publication Data
Hayes, Ann.
Meet the Marching Smithereens/written by
Ann Hayes; illustrated by Karmen Thompson.—1st ed.
p. cm.
ISBN 0-15-253158-0
1. Marching bands—Juvenile literature. 2. Musical
instruments—Juvenile literature. [1. Bands (Music)
2. Musical instruments.]
I. Thompson, Karmen Effenberger, ill.   II. Title.
ML1300.H39 1995
784.8′3—dc20   94-11896

First edition   A B C D E

Printed in Singapore

The illustrations in this book were done
in watercolor on Crescent watercolor board.
The display type and text type were set in
ITC Souvenir by Harcourt Brace & Company
Photocomposition Center, San Diego, California.
Color separations by Bright Arts, Ltd., Singapore
Printed and bound by Tien Wah Press, Singapore
This book was printed with soya-based inks
on Leykam recycled paper, which contains more
than 20 percent postconsumer waste and has
a total recycled content of at least 50 percent.
Production supervision by Warren Wallerstein and Kent MacElwee
Designed by Camilla Filancia

For our husbands, RUSSELL HAYES
and BARI THOMPSON, with gratitude
for their patience and devotion.

THE MARCHING
SMITHEREENS

Along the block and down the street, people wait
and listen. The far-off thump of the drums grows louder, keeping
a steady beat as the parade nears. *Budder-ump, budder-ump,
boom, boom, boom!* A cheer goes up from the crowd.

"Here comes the band!"
"Here come the Marching Smithereens!"

drum major

The drum major struts in front of the band. With her mace,
she beats time and sets the pace for the Marching Smithereens.
She uses hand signals and whistle blasts to say,

turn!

halt!

march!

play!

trombone

Make way for the majestic trombones! Their long slides move in and out, making the notes glide up and down. Trombones, part of the brass section, often lead the march because the slides need extra room.

trumpet

A brass instrument is made of a mouthpiece, a tube, and a cone that is shaped like a bell. The trumpet is mostly tube, making its voice brash and bright. Its thrilling notes often carry the melody.

mellophone

The mellophone is mostly cone. Its voice is as soft and blurred as yours when you open your mouth wide and say "ahhh" to the doctor. Its mellow sound makes the music full and round.

sousaphone

The largest horns have the lowest voices.
The sousaphone, the bullfrog of the band, was
invented by John Philip Sousa, a famous
composer of band music. It has the widest throat
and the biggest bell of all the brass, grumping and
groaning with a deep *umm-pa, umm-pa, umm-pa-pa.*
The tube circles the musician's body like a serpent.
The bell rises overhead like a giant golden bloom.

snare drum

Drums keep the beat set by the drum major. They march near the center of the band so that all the other players can hear the rhythm.

The snare drummer strikes the drum with wooden sticks. The beats sizzle and snap with a *ratta-tat, ratta-tat, tic-tic-tac!* You can also play on the rim with a sharp *clickety-clack!*

tom-toms

Tom-toms are a set of small drums that vary in size and pitch. The drummer plays different notes by beating from one drum to the next with bouncing sticks.

cymbals

Cymbals, thin metal plates, are clashed together or struck with a drumstick. Hear them resound with a *clang! crash! smash!,* adding zest and flash to the music.

bass drum

The bass drum, by far the biggest drum, can be hit on both sides with a mallet. Its deep, steady *boom, boom, boom* is the pulse of the march.

clarinet

The woodwinds—clarinet, flute, piccolo, and saxophone—are the acrobats of the band. Their quick notes frolic among the heavier voices of the brass.

The clarinet, like a yodeler, skips and skedaddles up and down the scale.

flute
& piccolo

Flute and piccolo players blow across an air hole, the way you play an empty bottle by blowing across its rim. The silver flute twitters and trills. The shrill notes of the piccolo, a pocket-size flute, dance on a tightrope above all the other instruments.

saxophone

The snazzy saxophone, "sax" for short, has many moods. In its jazz mood, a carefree sax plays rings around a tune. In the marching band, it often sounds hoarse and strong, like the bray of a donkey. You can easily recognize the sax by its turned-up bell.

bell-lyra

The bell-lyra is like a small keyboard
in the shape of a lyre. It has metal bars
of different lengths and often plays
the melody. When you strike the bars
with a mallet, sparkling notes chime out.

Down the street and round the bend—

the Smithereens march back again!

The Marching Smithereens have passed.
The crowd heads home, still feeling
that steady beat.

Budder-ump,

budder-ump,

boom,

boom,

boom . . .

It won't be long until the next parade, when the crowd will cheer,
"Here comes the band!"
"Here come the Marching Smithereens!"